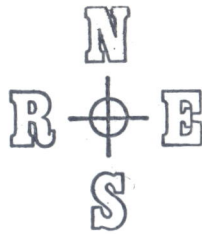

N
R ◆ E
S

THE WESTHILL PROJECT R.E. 5–16

MUSLIMS

3

GARTH READ
JOHN RUDGE

Muslim consultants

Rashida Sharif
Ghulam Mustafa Draper

M·G·P

MARY GLASGOW PUBLICATIONS

Published by Mary Glasgow Publications Limited,
Avenue House, 131–133 Holland Park Avenue,
London W11 4UT.

Typeset in Great Britain by Anneset,
Weston-super-Mare
Printed in Great Britain by W S Cowell Ltd,
Ipswich

British Library Cataloguing in Publication Data

Read, Garth
  Muslims.
  3
  1. Islam — For schools
  I. Title II. Rudge, John III. Series
  297

ISBN 1–85234–075–4

Acknowledgements

The authors and publishers are grateful to the following for permission to use copyright
material:

Photographs

Cover:
Jerry Wooldridge, I.P.A. Picture Library (Ka'ba)

Inside pages:
Jerry Wooldridge pages 7, 10, 12, 15 (top), 16, 17, 18, 19, 26, 30, 31, 32, 33, 38, 40, 43, 60, 63
Camera Press page 6
Peter Sanders pages 15 (bottom), 24, 37, 56 (top), 58 (top)
I.P.A. Picture Library pages 39, 48, 56 (bottom), 57, 58 (bottom)

The illustrations are by Metin Salih and on pages 42, 44, 46 and 49 by Maggie Brand.

Text
English translations of passages from the Qur'an are taken from the text with notes by
S. Abul A'la Maududi, English rendering by Muhammad Akbar Muradpuri and 'Abdul
'Aziz Kamal, published in 1987 by Islamic Publications (PVT.) Limited, Lahore.
The text on pages 20–3 (sacrifice of Ismail), 49 (Adam comes to Arafat), 50–1 (Ismail and
the well of Zamzam) and 52–3 (rebuilding of the Ka'ba) is based on the versions of these
stories found in The Prophets by Syed Ali Ashraf, published by Hodder and Stoughton
Ltd. (1981).
The story of Muhammad's last pilgrimage (pages 54–5) is based on the version found in
The Life of the Prophet Muhammad by Leila Azzam and Aisha Gouverneur, published by
the Islamic Texts Society (1985).

Contents

Introduction

This book is a part of your R.E. course. You will be asked to use it when you are learning about some of the things that Muslims do to express their beliefs.

You may find some unusual words in this book. Your teacher will help you to understand them. You will also learn about ideas and practices which may be strange to you. Take time to understand them. Look for more information about them. Remember all Muslims do not believe and do the same things in exactly the same way. Be ready to understand the differences as well as the similarities.

Ask yourself and others questions about why people believe and do these things. It is also worth trying to understand what you believe and how your beliefs affect your behaviour. Learning about other people can help us to know them and ourselves a little better.

There are other books in this series. They help you to learn about people who belong to other religions. Perhaps they will also be a part of your R.E. course.

1 Muslim community life

What is a community?

'A community is a group of people who live near each other.'

'We have a Community Centre near us. It is used by anyone who wants to go to it. People meet in groups and clubs at the Centre.'

'A community is made up of people who like doing the same things.'

Each of these statements says something about the idea of community. Perhaps you may be able to add some more ideas about what a community is and list some different communities to which you belong.

A community of communities

What is a community of communities? Perhaps these examples will help you find an answer.

Your city, town or village is a community of communities.

Your country is a community of communities.

Our world is a community of communities.

A community of communities exists when groups of different people have something important in common which links them together. It happens when many small communities are linked together in one large community.

The people who belong to a community of communities may have different coloured skins. They may speak different languages. They may wear different kinds of clothes. They may eat different kinds of food. They may enjoy different activities.

The members of a community of communities may be linked together because they
- come from the same country,
- play the same sport,
- like the same kind of music,
- share the same beliefs.

Every religion is a community of communities. The millions of people who belong to each religion are very different from each other. They may live in different countries. They may have different coloured skins. They may speak different languages. They may practise their religion in different ways.

Each religion is a community of communities because it links together lots of different people in one community. All these people are linked together because they have something very important in common.

The Muslim community of communities

Muslims belong to a community of communities. Some Muslims are British. Others are Pakistani, Turkish, African, Arabian, or Malaysian. And there are many others. The Muslim community is made up of different people living in different parts of the world.

Perhaps you could share with others in your class what you already know about Muslim people and about the things they have in common.

Ummah

The word ummah is the Arabic word which Muslims use to describe the Islamic community around the world. Muslims in different countries all belong to the ummah and all these different people try to live according to the beliefs and practices of Islam.

> They believe in Allah.
> They believe that many thousands of prophets have tried to teach people the way of Allah.
> They also believe that Muhammad is Allah's final prophet who gave them the Qur'an.
> They believe that the Qur'an is the perfect record of Allah's commands for all people.
> They try to keep the five basic duties of a Muslim and live their lives according to the highest standard of Islamic teaching.

Now you are the best community which has been raised up for the guidance of mankind: you enjoin what is right and forbid what is wrong and believe in Allah.

Surah 3:110

كُنتُمْ خَيْرَ أُمَّةٍ أُخْرِجَتْ لِلنَّاسِ تَأْمُرُونَ بِالْمَعْرُوفِ وَتَنْهَوْنَ عَنِ الْمُنكَرِ وَتُؤْمِنُونَ بِاللَّهِ

This verse from the Qur'an says something about the Islamic ummah and what it must try to do for all people. Perhaps you could talk to your friends about the ideas of community contained in these words.

Local Muslim communities

For most Muslims a mosque is the central focus of their community life. A mosque is the place where Muslims gather together and where they learn about their religion. It is a place of prayer.

Each local Muslim community is a part of the ummah. All the things that Muslims do together in the mosque help them to live according to the beliefs of Islam and show that they belong to the ummah.

On the next page there is a description of the programme of one busy local Muslim community in Britain. Some of you may belong to a community like this. If so, perhaps you could tell your friends about it.

The Sparkbrook Islamic Centre

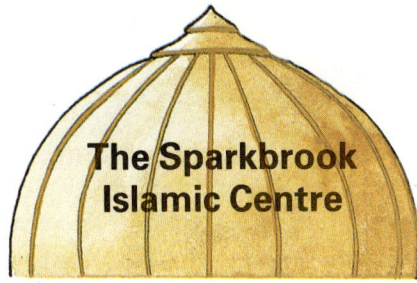

The Sparkbrook Islamic Centre in Birmingham is one example of a local Muslim community in Britain.

Most of the Muslims who belong to·the community are of Asian origin. Most of them came from Pakistan and India to live in England. Many of the younger members were born in England.

The Centre provides a wide range of activities for the Muslims and other people who live in the area.

The Sparkbrook Centre is a mosque. Its central feature is a large prayer hall. The five daily prayers are performed in this hall. Large numbers of Muslims gather for the congregational prayer on Fridays and for the special 'eid' prayers and celebrations during the year.

The Centre has its own Islamic school. This is called the Madrasah. Children and young people go to the Madrasah each afternoon. They learn to read Arabic and to recite the words of the Qur'an. Many children learn several languages, such as Arabic, English or Urdu, at the Madrasah.

The Centre also has a hostel, where people visiting Birmingham from different parts of England or the rest of the world can live. Many of these people join in the prayer and other activities which take place at the Centre.

The staff at the Centre also offer help and advice to people in difficulties. Many newly arrived people do not understand many of the customs and requirements of living in England. Others have no work and very little money. Some people do not know how to get help from doctors, dentists, police and teachers. The Centre's welfare service helps people solve some of these problems.

Muslims belonging to the Centre can find lots of books and magazines about Islam and other activities which interest them. There is a bookshop and a library and also a Day Centre for the old and the lonely. There are clubs for boys and girls. Sometimes members of these clubs join with members of other clubs in the area for sporting and other recreational activities.

The Muslim community at Sparkbrook also gives a warm welcome to groups of school pupils and teachers. They come to visit the Centre to learn about the mosque, about Islam, and about the Muslim way of life. This helps them to understand what it means to be a Muslim and to respect people with different beliefs and customs from their own.

Prayer at the mosque

Of course there is an enormous number of local mosques in the world. Each has its own distinctive appearance and its own programme of activities. In all cases, regular prayer is the most important activity at a mosque. This is because praying five times each day is one of the duties which every Muslim tries to perform.

In most mosques, the midday prayer on Fridays is very important. It is called Jum'ah, which in English means 'the day of general assembly'. Most Muslims try to get to the mosque for this prayer, so each mosque is usually crowded for this time of prayer on Fridays.

Some groups require 40 Muslims to be present before this group prayer can take place. Others do not mind how many or how few people are there. However, most Muslims think it is their duty to join in this weekly prayer. It is a way of following the practice of Muhammad and of showing that each Muslim belongs to the worldwide Islamic ummah.

Supporting the community

Muslims are required to give money or some other share of their wealth to the Islamic community. This regular giving of money is known as Zakat. It too is part of each local Muslim community and is another of the five duties which all Muslims seek to carry out.

The money is used to support the local community, advance the cause of Islam and help poor and needy people. In some Muslim communities the Zakat must be paid to the authorities, who then decide how it should be used. Other groups encourage individuals to give their Zakat directly to the people who need or deserve it.

Most Muslims agree that they should make sure that they have paid all legal debts and cared properly for their families and other dependants, before they pay the Zakat. To help them to do this most Muslim teaching suggests that two and a half per cent of what is left after caring for one's dependants, is a good guide to the amount of Zakat that should be paid.

Some communities have detailed rules about what each member should pay as their Zakat. The schedule below is one example of such rules.

SCHEDULE OF ZAKAT

Wealth on which Zakat is payable	Minimum amount owned before Zakat is paid	Rate of Zakat
1 Agricultural produce	5 Awsuq (653 kg) per harvest	5% of produce in case of irrigated land; 10% of produce from rain-fed land
2 Gold, silver, ornaments of gold and silver	85 grams of gold or 595 grams of silver	2.5% of value
3 Cash in hand or at bank	Value of 595 grams of silver	2.5% of amount
4 Trading goods	Value of 595 grams of silver	2.5% of value of goods
5 Cows and buffaloes	30 in number	For every 30, one 1-year-old; for every 40, one 2-year-old
6 Goats and sheep	40 in number	One for first 40; two for 120; three for 300; one more for every 100
7 Produce of mines	Any quantity	20% of value of produce
8 Camels	5 in number	a Up to 24, one sheep or goat for each five camels b 25–35, one 1-year-old she-camel c 36–45, one 2-year-old she-camel d 46–60, one 3-year-old she-camel e 61–75, one 4-year-old she-camel f 76–90, two 2-year-old she-camels g 91–120, two 3-year-old she-camels h 121 or more, one 2-year-old she-camel for each additional 40, or one 3-year-old she-camel for each additional 50

(from: *Islam, Belief and Teachings*, by Ghulam Sarwar, The Muslim Educational Trust, 1980, page 75.)

13

Of course, many Muslims give away much more of their wealth to help the poor and needy than just what is required as Zakat. Muslim teaching encourages people to be generous and caring. For many Muslims, just doing one's duty is not enough. They look for other ways to give to charity and to support the Muslim community.

For example, opportunities to give extra money and support for needy people are important parts of the special celebrations which take place at the mosque from time to time.

For most Muslims, paying Zakat and other acts of charity are ways of worshipping and obeying Allah. They are ways of showing their belief that everything they have belongs to Allah. They are ways of helping them not to be selfish and greedy. By giving generously to support the community and help needy people, they believe that they are pleasing Allah and obeying his commands.

﷽ إِنَّمَا ٱلصَّدَقَٰتُ لِلْفُقَرَآءِ وَٱلْمَسَٰكِينِ وَٱلْعَٰمِلِينَ عَلَيْهَا وَٱلْمُؤَلَّفَةِ قُلُوبُهُمْ وَفِى ٱلرِّقَابِ وَٱلْغَٰرِمِينَ وَفِى سَبِيلِ ٱللَّهِ وَٱبْنِ ٱلسَّبِيلِ فَرِيضَةً مِّنَ ٱللَّهِ وَٱللَّهُ عَلِيمٌ حَكِيمٌ

As a matter of fact, alms are only for the needy and the indigent, and for those who are employed to collect them and for those whose hearts are to be won over and for the ransoming of slaves and for helping the debtors and for the Way of Allah and for the hospitality of the way-farers. This is an obligatory duty from Allah: and Allah is All-Knowing, All-Wise.

Surah 9:60

Celebrating festivals in the community

Muslims have two important celebrations each year. These celebrations are sometimes called festivals. The Arabic word for festival is eid.

One festival is called Eid ul Fitr. Eid ul Fitr takes place at the end of the month of Ramadan. At this festival Muslims give thanks for the benefits they gained from fasting during daylight hours in the month of Ramadan.

Perhaps you know that keeping this fast is another of the five duties of a Muslim. Muslims call this duty of fasting during Ramadan by the Arabic name, Saum.

The second major festival is called Eid ul Adha. This festival is celebrated at the time of the Hajj, during the month of Dhu'l Hijjah.

The Hajj is the pilgrimage to Makkah. This pilgrimage takes place each year and it too is one of the five duties of a Muslim. Most Muslims try to go on this pilgrimage at least once in their life.

In the picture you can see some Muslims celebrating this festival at Regent's Park mosque in London.

ISLAMIC CALENDAR 1987 1407/8 AH

DIFFERENT CALENDARS

Muslims began their numbering of the years from the time when the Prophet Muhammad and his companions migrated from Makkah to Medina.

It is generally agreed that this took place in the year 622 CE. The letters CE stand for Common Era. This suggests that this is the system of numbering the years most commonly used throughout the world today. This numbering begins from what was believed to be the date of the birth of Jesus Christ.

There is therefore a difference of 622 years between the numbering used by Muslims and the numbering used in the Common Era calendar. The Islamic calendar is lunar. This means that its months are fixed by the position of the moon and not by the sun, as is the case with the Common Era calendar. There are twelve months in the Islamic calendar and each is either 30 or 29 days, depending on the position of the moon.

Eid ul Fitr

Eid ul Fitr, the festival of fast-breaking, is a time for thanksgiving and happiness after the month-long fast of Ramadan. On this day, Muslims do many of the kinds of things which people do when they celebrate.

They join with their families and friends to eat some of their favourite foods.

They may wear their best clothes or buy new ones.

They may give each other greeting cards and other presents.

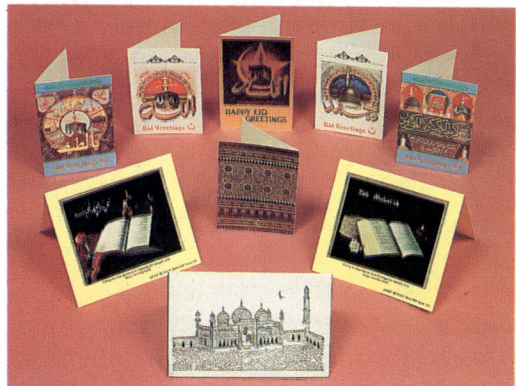

For Muslims, the times for prayer at the mosque are also very special during Eid ul Fitr.

Ramadan

Of course, this day of celebration and thanksgiving is mainly about the fast of Ramadan. Without the fast and other events of Ramadan, there would not be any Eid ul Fitr. Ramadan is the name for the ninth month in the Islamic calendar.

Going without food and drink during daylight hours is the central feature of Ramadan. All Muslims, except children under twelve, women in the late stages of pregnancy or those who are travelling or ill, are obliged to join in this fast.

Remembering and giving thanks to Allah for revealing the Qur'an to the Prophet Muhammad is also an important part of Ramadan.

One night during the month of Ramadan is specially important. It is known as the 'Night of Power'. While there is some doubt about which night should be recognised as the 'Night of Power', most Muslims observe it on the 27th day of Ramadan. On this night some Muslims stay awake all night to offer prayer and to read the Qur'an. It is the night, above all others, when Muslims express their beliefs about the Qur'an and how it came to be written.

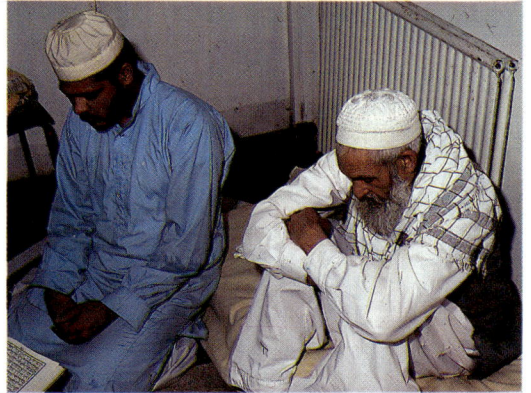

During the last few nights of Ramadan, some Muslims separate themselves from the rest of the community. They are said to be in i'tikaf or retreat. People in i'tikaf may spend all day and most of the night reading or reciting the Qur'an. This too is a way of showing how important the Qur'an is to Muslims.

Remembering and giving thanks for Allah's goodness in providing food is also an important part of Ramadan.

After sunset on each day of Ramadan, those who are keeping the fast break their fast with a light meal. Some go to the mosque to share this meal with others. Many Muslims break their fast by drinking a glass of water and eating a few dates. According to some traditions this is how the Prophet Muhammad broke his fast. This light meal, each evening of Ramadan, is called iftar. The iftar is a way of satisfying hunger and thirst and of showing thanks for Allah's goodness and mercy.

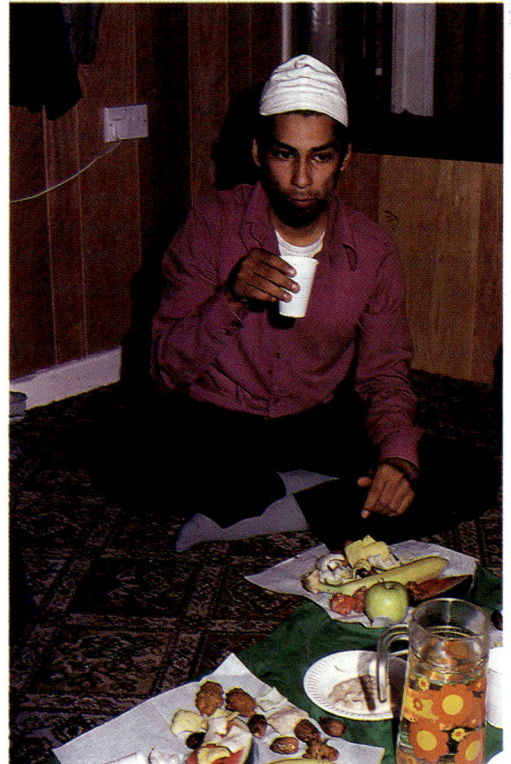

Giving money is also a part of Ramadan. During this month, Muslims keep their duty of Zakat. This too is one of the five pillars of Islam. Most Muslims try to pay their Zakat before the end of Ramadan and before the beginning of Eid ul Fitr. Some Muslims give extra money as a way of celebrating this festival. This money is used to help people in need.

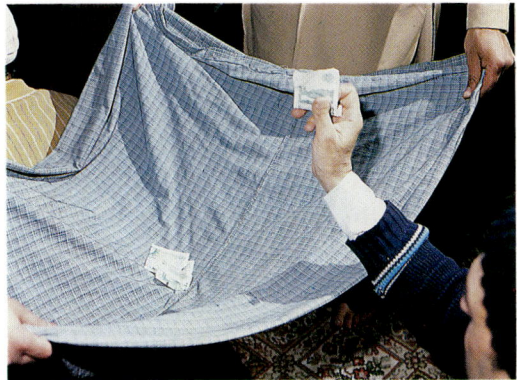

BELIEFS

All the activities of Ramadan and Eid ul Fitr give Muslims a chance to express some of the important beliefs of Islam.

- Belief in God is central to everything that Muslims do. During Ramadan and Eid ul Fitr, Muslims express the belief that there is no god but Allah and that Muhammad is Allah's messenger.

- Beliefs in the goodness and mercy of Allah are also expressed in this festival. At Ramadan Muslims are reminded that Allah has given them the Qur'an and provides for all their needs.

- Events such as those linked to the 'Night of Power', express the belief that the Qur'an was revealed by Allah to Muhammad. They believe, therefore, that it must be kept in its original form and language.

- In keeping Saum and Zakat, Muslims show their belief that submission to the will of Allah is the only way to lasting peace.

- Muslims believe that fasting helps develop their self-discipline. It helps them not to be greedy and selfish. It also helps them to care for hungry and needy people.

Eid ul Adha

The second important festival or eid, celebrated by Muslim communities around the world, is called Eid ul Adha, the Festival of Sacrifice. Eid ul Adha begins on the tenth day of the month of Dhu'l Hijjah. It lasts for three days.

This eid is based on part of the story of the Prophet Ibrahim. Muslims believe that Ibrahim lived many thousands of years before Muhammad. He had two sons called Ismail and Ishaq. They believe that Muhammad was a descendant of Ismail.

As you read this version of part of the story of Ibrahim, written for Muslim children, notice the Muslim practice of repeating the words 'peace be on him' when the prophet Ibrahim's name is used. Perhaps you could find out why Muslims do this.

The Sacrifice of Ismail

Ibrahim (peace be on him) was one of the prophets of Allah. He had two sons whose names were Ismail and Ishaq. Soon after Ismail was born, he and his mother had to leave Ibrahim's home in Canaan. They went to live a long way away from there, in the city which is now called Makkah.

When Ismail was still young, Ibrahim (peace be on him) dreamt that he was ordered by Allah to sacrifice his most precious thing. As Ismail was the person he loved most he believed that Allah wanted him to sacrifice his son, Ismail.

He travelled from Canaan to the place where Ismail and his mother, Hagar, lived. There, he told Ismail of his dream. Ismail said, 'O my father, do as you have been ordered to do. If this is what Allah has commanded you to do, I am ready.'

Ibrahim (peace be on him) told his son to bring a cord and a knife and they both went to Mount Thabir.

On the way Shaytan came to them in the shape of a man and said to Ibrahim (peace be on him), 'You must have seen Shaytan in your dream telling you to cut the throat of your son.'

Ibrahim (peace be on him) threw a stone at him and said, 'Go away! You are the enemy of all who seek to obey Allah.'

Shaytan then turned to Ismail and said, 'Do you know, my child, that your father says that Allah has told him to cut your throat?'

The child said, 'Yes, let Allah's will be done. Go away.' And he threw a stone at him.

Shaytan again tried to persuade him not to go. But Ismail was angry and took many stones and started throwing them at him.

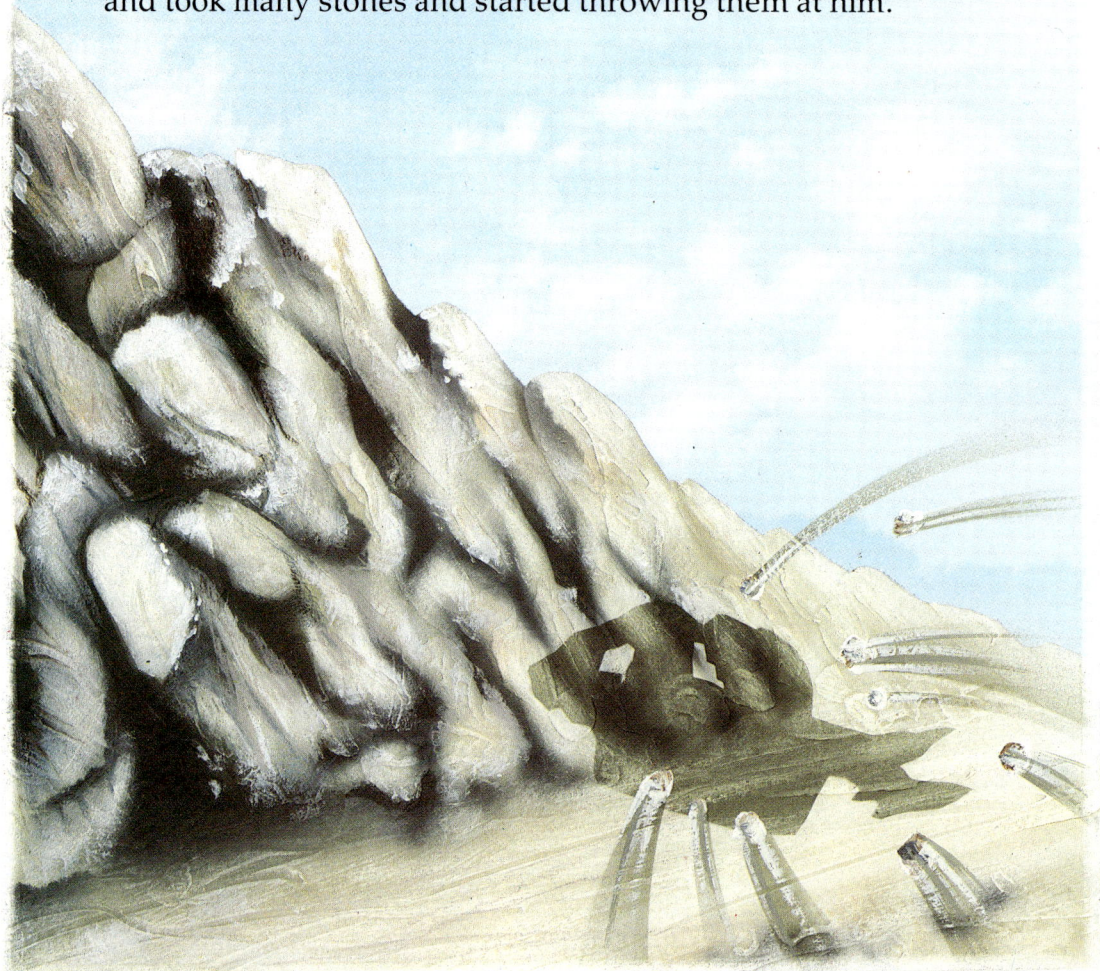

Shaytan then went to Hagar and said, 'O mother of Ismail, Ibrahim will kill your son.'

'No,' she said, 'he loves him.'

'But,' Shaytan said, 'he says it is Allah's order.'

'Then,' she said, 'let what Allah has ordered be done.'

Shaytan was defeated by the strength of their faith.

Ibrahim (peace be on him) and Ismail left their home and climbed to the top of Mount Thabir. Ismail said, 'Tie my hands and feet so that I cannot move and so that my blood does not gush over you. Turn me on my face so that you are not moved by love.'

Then when Ibrahim (peace be on him) was about to make the sacrifice, Allah said, 'O Ibrahim, you have acted according to your dream. But you must not sacrifice your son. We therefore give you a victim in place of your son.'

Ibrahim (peace be on him) who had shut his eyes, opened them and saw a big ram. It ran down the hill to Mina where they caught it and sacrificed it.

After sacrificing the ram, Ibrahim (peace be on him) took Ismail back to his mother and he went back to his home and the rest of his family in Canaan.

Eid ul Adha is a time for celebration. It is a time for special prayer and other activities at the mosque and in homes.

One special activity during this festival is to kill an animal, in a ritual way, for food. Muslims do this to remember the part in the story where Ibrahim was willing to sacrifice his son, Ismail. This helps them to remember their belief that they should be ready to sacrifice everything, even their lives, in order to obey Allah.

In some countries, this ritual killing of the animal for food may happen in a public place. Large numbers of the Muslim community may be present to watch or join in this ritual. In other countries such as Britain, the animal is more likely to be killed at the local Muslim butcher's. In both cases, the meat is usually divided into three portions. One portion is given to poor people. Another is offered as a gift to friends and relatives. The third portion is kept by the family.

Many Muslims also give money to the poor and needy of the world during Eid ul Adha. This too is a sacrifice because they are giving up something for other people. Many Muslims also see this sacrificial giving of money to help others as a way of worshipping and obeying Allah. It is a gift of money over and above what is required by the duty of Zakat.

BELIEFS

Three important Islamic beliefs are expressed through the celebration of Eid ul Adha.

- The story of Ibrahim illustrates for Muslims their belief that obedience to Allah must be more important than anything else.

- Many Muslims believe that they can know the will of Allah and that nothing should stop them carrying it out.

- The story of Ibrahim and the annual celebration of Eid ul Adha reminds Muslims of their belief that it is better to give up everything for Allah than to be greedy and interested only in themselves.

2 Muslim family life

All these houses look the same. They are made of similar bricks and mortar. They are about the same size, probably with the same number of rooms. Each has a small garden.

But these houses are not all the same.

> Some of the doors and windows are painted different colours.
> They may be decorated in different ways inside.
> They may have different kinds of furniture in them.
> Some may be warm and dry: some may be cold and damp.

What makes them all different is the people who live in them. It is the people who live there who make each house their own home.

Some people suggest that a house becomes a home when the people who live there feel:

- that they belong to one another,
- comfortable in familiar surroundings,
- that they are wanted and valued by each other,
- that they can be themselves,
- that they can share important things together,
- that they can support one another in good and bad times.

You may like to share with others your ideas about what turns a house into a home. Do all the items in your list and the one above apply to people who live alone?

Imram comes home

I'm Imram. I'm 15 and I live in Longsight in Manchester. Our house is not very posh, because we're not very well off. My dad was out of work for a long time. But I like it here. We're a really close family, and I feel at home here.

I like it best on a really cold day in winter when I get home from school. I'm normally frozen, and tired out too. When I push open the front door, it's all warm and friendly and familiar inside. My little sister comes running up to me and gives me a big hug. My younger brother usually pretends not to notice me, but he soon wants to know what I've been up to. My mum calls out from the kitchen, 'That you, Imram? Don't forget to take your shoes off.' Then I know I'm home. We have to take our shoes off because Mum keeps the front room spotless.

I usually go and chat to my mum. There's always a fantastic smell coming from the kitchen. Then I go up to my room till Dad comes home. Because I'm the eldest one at home (my older brother is working for my uncle in London) I have a room of my own. I like it when I can just be myself. Sometimes I listen to music, or read a book, or just lie on the bed. I have everything where I want it – my pictures, an old music centre my dad bought me from the market, a great big Asian rug hanging on the wall (my grandad gave me that) and my books on the shelves on the wall. I read all sorts. On the top shelf I keep my copy of the Qur'an. It's our most important book. It has a special place.

When my dad comes home, everything stops because it's time for our family prayers. We all get together in the front room – the one Mum keeps so clean. That's where we always pray. Dad doesn't say much and we all keep quiet. I used to be very scared of him, because he's very strict with us. But I know he loves us and cares about us a lot – and sometimes he winks at me, because I'm the oldest son at home.

When we have our prayers, Dad goes out in front. We all face one of the walls with a small carpet hanging on it. It's got a picture of the Ka'ba on it. If anybody is talking, Dad just looks round at us. He doesn't say anything. We all know what he means. When we have our prayers, I go just behind Dad, then my brother, then Mum and my sister. Dad says, 'Allahu Akbar'. Then we know the prayers have begun. It means 'God is Most Great'. I'd always said these words since I was a little boy, but I didn't really understand what they meant till I was older.

When prayers are over, we all relax before we have our evening meal. Mum does some great food. We nearly always have Asian food, hot and spicy. It's much more interesting to eat than school dinner – chips, chips and more chips. We all sit round on a big rug on the floor and Mum puts the food out on a small table in the middle. I get so hungry, but we all have to sit there till everything's ready. Then Dad says some words from the Qur'an. He keeps telling us we should be thankful for our food.

After our meal I usually go off to the Madrasah. When you're feeling all warm and full up, and it's freezing outside, it's a bit of a drag. But I don't mind really. I see all my mates there.

I love our home. I'd hate it if anything happened and we had to move. But I suppose I'd get used to it, because we'd still be all together. I remember there was a time when I used to feel embarrassed about our home. When I went to some of my friends' houses they weren't like ours. We don't have tables and chairs and lots of pictures on the wall like they do, and we eat different food. But now I'm proud I come from a Muslim home. I'm glad I belong to a family like ours, and I like it when some of my friends come round and meet my family.

Muslim homes

For most Muslims, their house is an important place for expressing their religion. Their houses may look much the same as other houses near them. However, when you go inside, you may find lots of things which tell you that the people living there belong to the religion of Islam. You may find a copy of the Qur'an in a very prominent place, perhaps on a high shelf near the door.

Many Muslims take off their shoes as they enter the front door of their house. All visitors will also be asked to remove their shoes before entering the house. This is because they believe that their house is a mosque, as well as a home. For Muslims, any clean place, where people perform the five daily prayers facing towards the city of Makkah, is a mosque.

Taking off shoes helps to keep the floors clean. It is also believed to be a mark of respect to Allah. By thinking of their home in this way, Muslims are reminded that they should live all of their life according to the will of Allah.

Prayer

One of the five duties of a Muslim is to pray at five different times each day. Most of these prayers are performed at home and usually the whole family joins in.

At least one room in the house is arranged so that these prayers can take place in a proper way. A compass will be used to find the direction of the city of Makkah. A quotation from the Qur'an or other suitable sign may be placed on the wall to mark this direction. Small colourful prayer mats may be placed on the floor to make sure that the place of prayer is as clean as possible.

One member of the family, usually the father, leads the prayer. Other members of the family and visiting guests arrange themselves in straight lines behind the leader of the prayer.

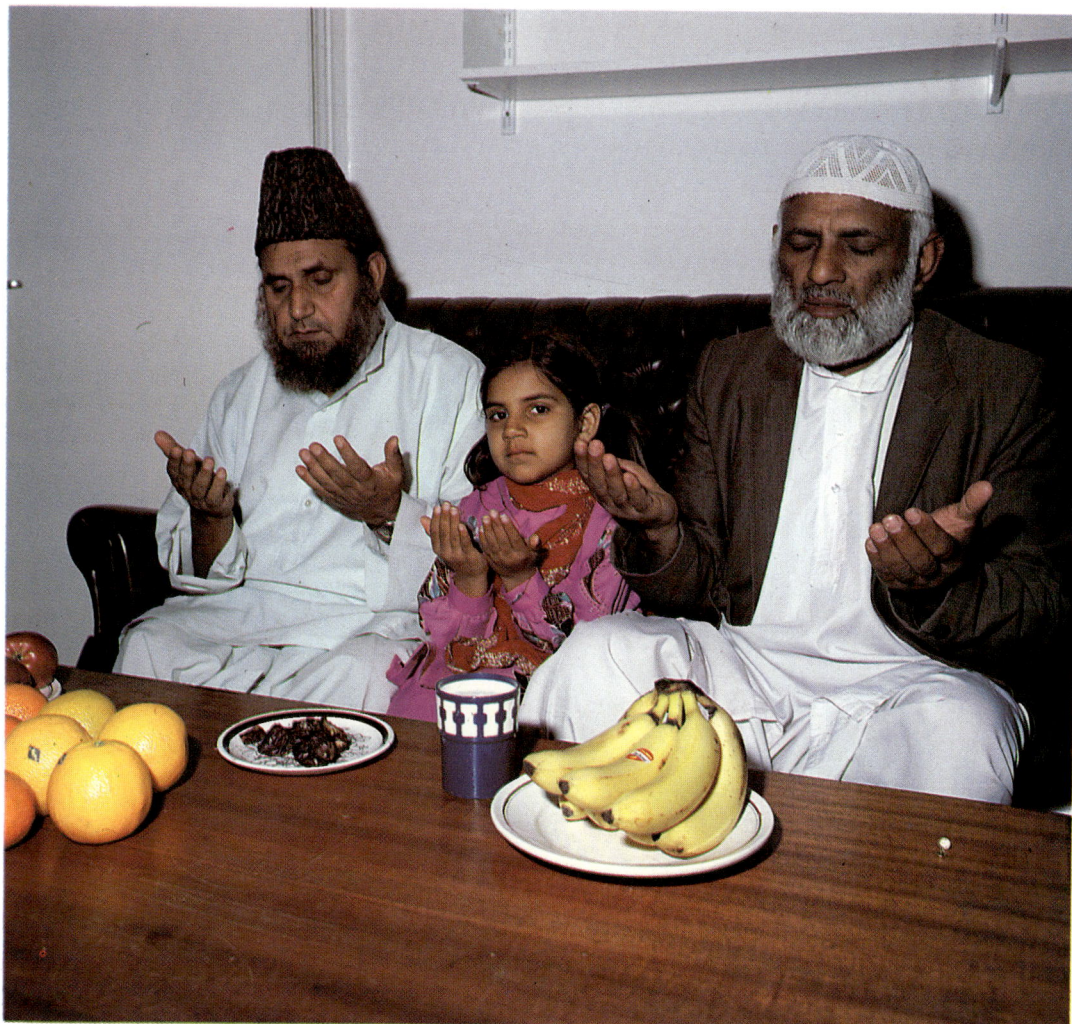

Some Muslim families offer prayers before they eat their meals. This may be a very simple form of prayer where everyone says the Arabic words of the Bismillah. In English this means, 'In the name of Allah, most Gracious, most Merciful'. On some occasions, there may be a longer time of prayer and reciting parts of the Qur'an.

Offering prayer in the home is another way of expressing Islamic belief. It shows that the family seeks to obey Allah and believes that Allah has provided all the good things that they enjoy.

Reading the Qur'an

The reading or reciting of the Qur'an may also be an important part of Muslim family life.

Some families read from the Qur'an either just before or just after one of the five daily prayers. During this time, younger children learn to start reading the Qur'an in Arabic. Others may have it read to them in their own language. Some families have small story books about Muhammad and other Muslim prophets. These, too, may be read to younger members of the family.

By thinking of their homes as mosques, Muslim families express their belief that they are a part of the worldwide Islamic ummah. The little community of their family is a part of the much larger Islamic community of communities. Performing the prayer in exactly the same way as other Muslims in other parts of the world helps them feel that they belong to this larger community. They believe that by reading or reciting passages from the Qur'an they are linked together with all people who try to live in obedience to Allah.

Perhaps your family has some regular customs which you share in and enjoy. For some of you these may be similar to the Muslim practices described above. Some of you may belong to different religious traditions and others may not keep any religious traditions at all. If you talk with your friends about this side of family life, you may be surprised by how many different family customs there are, even among members of your class or school.

Muslims and death

Belonging to other people in a family is often the closest and most important relationship we develop. This is partly why a great deal of sadness and hurt may come when one member dies. On the other hand, belonging to a family can also be a source of comfort and caring whenever death does occur.

Many people are puzzled by death. It is so mysterious. Perhaps that is why beliefs about a possible life after death are so important to many people.

'I believe that when you die you go to heaven or hell. It all depends on whether you have been good or bad.'

'Death is horrible. I hated seeing my rabbit when it died. It didn't seem the same when it went all limp and lifeless.'

'I believe that you have to live a good life so that when you die you will come back again as a better person.'

'When your body dies, your soul or your spirit goes on. It goes on growing closer to God.'

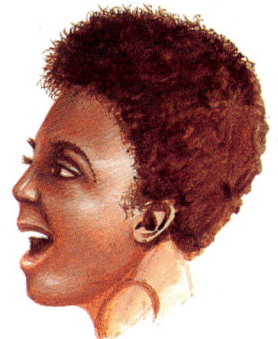

'When you're dead, you're dead. I don't think there's anything else.'

Perhaps you have your own ideas and beliefs about death and any after-life.

All the religions have beliefs and teachings about death. Are any of your beliefs about death part of a religious tradition?

Muslim funerals

Muslims believe in an after-life. They also believe in a Day of Judgement. This refers to a time when everybody will be rewarded or punished by Allah for the kind of life they have lived.

إِنَّا نَحْنُ نُحْىِ ٱلْمَوْتَىٰ وَنَكْتُبُ مَاقَدَّمُواْ وَءَاثَٰرَهُمْ وَكُلَّ شَىْءٍ أَحْصَيْنَٰهُ فِىٓ إِمَامٍ مُّبِينٍ

وَوُفِّيَتْ كُلُّ نَفْسٍ مَّا عَمِلَتْ وَهُوَ أَعْلَمُ بِمَا يَفْعَلُونَ

> We shall certainly one day raise the dead to life. We are recording all the deeds they have done and also that which they have left behind: We have preserved everything in an open Book.
>
> Surah 36:12

> And every living thing shall be recompensed fully for whatever it had done. Allah knows full well what the people do.
>
> Surah 39:70

When Muslims know that someone is dying, they may do several things to express these beliefs. Many believe that soon after death every person will be asked what they believe. If the central belief of Islam is heard just before death, the person will be better equipped to answer correctly. This is why the words of the Shahadah (see page 44) may be spoken in the ear of the dying person.

لَا إِلَٰهَ إِلَّا ٱللَّهُ مُحَمَّدٌ رَّسُولُ ٱللَّهِ

> There is no god but Allah, Muhammad is the Messenger of Allah.

Some Muslims may place the dying person facing in the direction of Makkah. The head may be raised to emphasise this looking in the direction of the Ka'ba in Makkah.

When a Muslim dies it is customary for relatives and friends to visit the dead person's family to comfort and help them. At this time there will be prayer and the reading of the Qur'an.

RITUAL WASHING

Ritual washing of the corpse is also part of a Muslim funeral. The body is washed at least three times. Special care is taken to follow the ritual washing which Muslims use as part of their preparation for prayer. Perfume is often placed in the hair and on those parts of the body used in the prayer ritual – hands, feet, knees and forehead.

DRESSING THE CORPSE

After being washed, the corpse is wrapped in a special shroud or other white material. If the dead person had made the pilgrimage to Makkah, the body may be wrapped in the special white garment worn by pilgrims during the visit to the Ka'ba.

Burial

Prayer is an important part of the burial ceremony. The prayer used is a special salah and it may take place at the home, at the mosque or at the cemetery. This special prayer includes reciting, four times, the words 'Allah is most great'. This prayer is led by an imam.

At the grave the imam recites the following words from the Qur'an.

> We have created you from this earth and We shall return you into it and then shall bring you forth out of it once again.
>
> Surah 20:55

مِنْهَا خَلَقْنَكُمْ وَفِيهَا نُعِيدُكُمْ وَمِنْهَا نُخْرِجُكُمْ تَارَةً أُخْرَىٰ ۞

These words help to explain why Muslims do not cremate their dead. They are taught always to bury their dead.

The corpse is then placed on its side in the grave so that it faces towards the city of Makkah.

A Muslim grave is usually very simple, often with just a stone at the head of the grave. This is because Muslims believe that all people are equal before Allah, and that it is wrong to suggest that some are greater than others.

In Muslim history there have been many famous monuments to leaders and rulers. The best known is the Taj Mahal in India, which was built as a tomb for Shah Jahan and his wife.

According to Muslim teaching, however, this sort of practice is wrong. It may lead people to think more of the person who has died than of Allah who alone should be honoured and worshipped.

Mourning

There are many customs dealing with the period of mourning following a death. These customs vary from country to country and between different groups of Muslims. Sometimes Muslims observe a fixed period of time for mourning. During this time they may give food or other gifts to the poor and needy. They may set aside special times for reciting the Qur'an at home.

When a person dies, the period of preparation, burial and mourning is important for Muslims. During this time, all the rituals, prayers and readings are intended to show special respect for the person who has died.

During this time, Muslims also remember their belief that Allah is very great. They must therefore prepare themselves to come near to Allah. Death is the time when all people come very near to Allah. The reciting of the Shahadah, the ritual washing of the corpse, and the other funeral customs are all part of this preparation.

Death is usually a sad time for all people. Muslims, too, feel sad when a member of their family or a close friend dies. They are taught, however, that they should not allow this grief to upset them so much that they forget their belief that all things, including death, are the will of Allah, who is compassionate and merciful.

3 Muslim personal life

What I would like to be

Most of us, when we are young, think about what we might be like when we are older. We wonder what we might look like. We wonder where we might be. We wonder what we might be doing.

Of course, we can never be sure what might happen to us in the future. However, we can think about some of the things we would like to be or do in the future.

I want to be like my mum.
I want to fly to Mars.
I want to have a good time
I want to be a famous ice-skater.
I want to find a cure for cancer.
I want to be alone on a desert island.
I want to be rich and powerful.
I want to stop people being cruel to animals.

Perhaps you may be able to talk to your friends about some of the things you would like to do or be in the future.

Most of the world's religions teach people that whatever their personal ambitions and interests might be, the will of God must come before all else. These religions also teach people how to discover and obey the will of God and therefore to become the kinds of people they believe God wants them to be.

What Muslims would like to be

Muslims, like everyone else, think about what they would like to do or be in the future. They are taught that all of their personal interests and wishes must reflect the will of Allah. They must be faithful servants of Allah before everything else. Whatever they may wish to be or do they must strive to serve Allah. To help them to do this the religion of Islam teaches Muslims to build their personal lives around five special duties. Muslims are taught that if they keep these duties throughout their lives, they will be obeying Allah and will become the kind of people that Allah loves and rewards.

The five pillars of Islam

These five duties are often called the 'five pillars' of Islam. Pillars are large, strong posts which hold up buildings or bridges. When Muslims speak about these duties as 'pillars', they are saying that their whole way of life is supported by them.

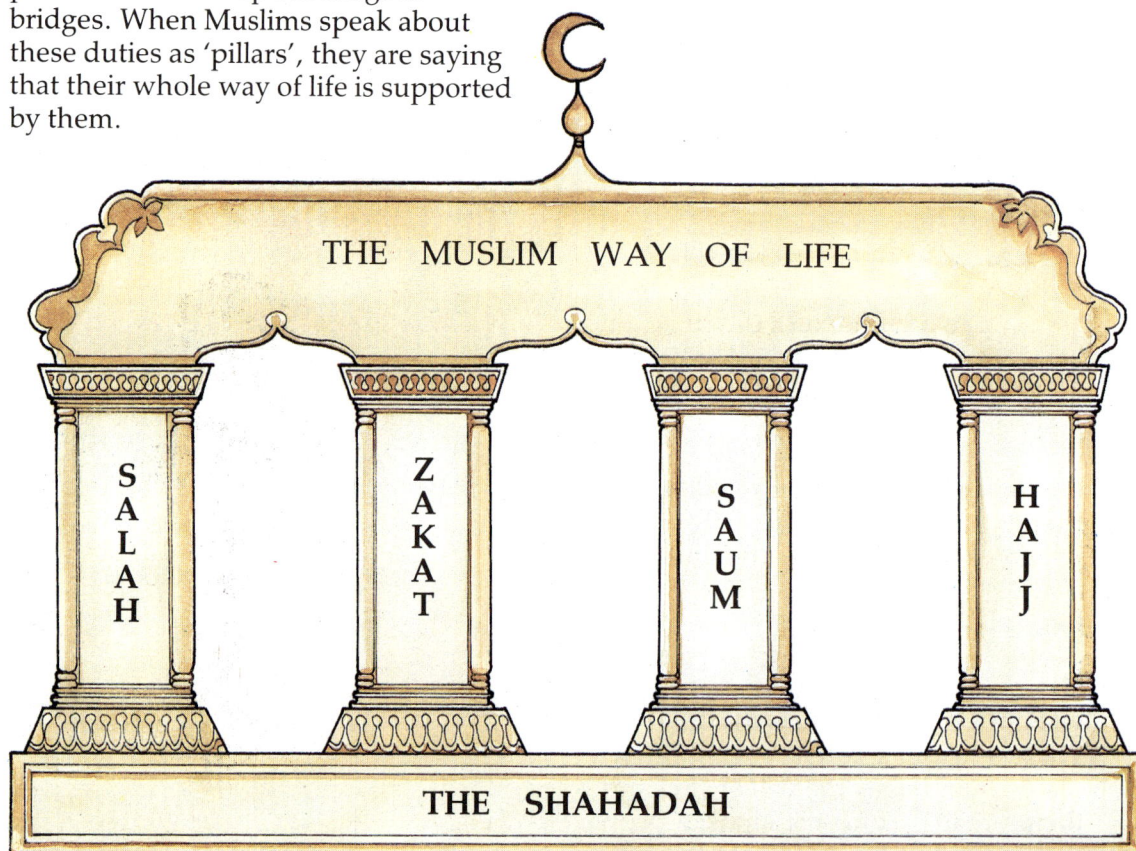

THE MUSLIM WAY OF LIFE

SALAH   ZAKAT   SAUM   HAJJ

THE SHAHADAH

There are two aspects to each of these five duties. These are:

- rituals which must be performed in the correct way,
- personal beliefs and attitudes which must be shared by those joining in the regular rituals.

Performing each ritual in the required way is seen by most Muslims to be one way of obeying Allah by following the practice of the Prophet Muhammad.

Muslims also believe that by carrying out these duties they are becoming the kind of people that Allah wants them to be.

For Muslims, however, the outward actions are useless, unless the people who perform them are sincere in their desire to obey and please Allah. While anyone can see Muslims performing the rituals, it is the teaching of Islam that only Allah knows how sincere each person is.

RITUALS

A ritual is a combination of actions and words which people do regularly.

Many religious rituals are intended to express particular beliefs. They also help believers to develop the kinds of character that the religion teaches to be desirable and valuable.

The five pillars of Islam

The religion of Islam teaches that keeping these five duties helps each Muslim to develop spiritually. This usually means that they are developing the personal qualities of character that Muslims believe are pleasing to Allah. In this chart and on the next two pages you will find some information about the five pillars of Islam. You should look carefully at both the required outward actions and the intended inner beliefs and attitudes.

DUTIES	OUTWARD ACTIONS
THE SHAHADAH	Reciting, as often as possible, the Arabic words which sum up the central beliefs of Islam. Here are the words of the Shahadah in Arabic and in English. لَا اِلٰهَ اِلَّا اللّٰه مُحَمَّدٌ رَّسُوْلُ اللّٰهِ *There is no god but Allah;* *Muhammad is the Messenger of Allah.*
SALAH	There are two parts to the Muslim ritual of prayer, after reciting the Bismillah. *Wudu* Washing various parts of the body in a set order: hands, mouth, nose, face, arms, head, feet. *Salah* Praying five times each day in the required way, standing, bowing, prostrating, and sitting. Many of the words recited during the prayer come from the Qur'an.

PERSONAL BELIEFS AND ATTITUDES

Believing in the oneness of Allah. Turning one's whole life towards Allah. Recognising that Allah is more important than anything else in life.

Believing in Muhammad as the final prophet of Allah.

Desiring to follow the example of Muhammad as closely as possible.

Wudu Intending to perform the duty of prayer properly.
Wanting to be properly prepared before approaching Allah in prayer.
Wanting to be free from all things which are against the will of Allah.

Salah Wanting to be aware of Allah throughout the day.
Showing reverence and respect in the presence of Allah.
Feeling humble in the presence of Allah.

DUTIES	OUTWARD ACTIONS
SAUM	Fasting during daylight hours in the month of Ramadan. Joining in regular prayer and in reading of the Qur'an. Giving money and performing other acts of charity.
ZAKAT	Paying a part of one's income and wealth, each year, to support the Muslim community.
HAJJ	Going on pilgrimage to the Ka'ba in Makkah at least once in a lifetime. Wearing the special clothes worn by all pilgrims. Performing various ceremonies and rituals in Makkah and other important places in the traditions of Islam.

PERSONAL BELIEFS AND ATTITUDES

Being grateful to Allah for all good things.
Exercising self-control over every part of one's life.
Wanting to be free from greed and selfishness.
Caring for people in need.

Being grateful to Allah for all good things.
Treating all of one's possessions as a gift from Allah.
Accepting some responsibility for supporting the Islamic ummah and people in need.

Being willing to sacrifice everything in obedience to Allah.
Feeling sorry for all failure to live in total obedience to Allah.
Wanting to follow the practice of Muhammad.
Feeling a part of the worldwide Islamic ummah.
Recognising that all Muslims are equal before Allah.

Hajj

The Hajj, or pilgrimage to the Ka'ba in Makkah, is one of the five pillars of Islam. Islam teaches that all adult Muslims who are able to observe this duty should go on this pilgrimage at least once in their lifetime.

Of course, large numbers of Muslims never manage to go on this pilgrimage. Such things as the difficulties and expense of long-distance travel, sickness, old age, handicaps, war and other things prevent many Muslims from making this journey. Some Muslim groups allow people to ask other people, or perhaps pay someone else, to go on the pilgrimage for them.

The Ka'ba

The Ka'ba is a cube-shaped building in the middle of the courtyard of the Great Mosque in the city of Makkah. It plays an important part in the activities and ceremonies of the Hajj.

On the next few pages you will find parts of three stories. In each of these stories there are some references to the Ka'ba. The retelling of these stories and acting out parts of them during the Hajj helps Muslims to understand the meaning and purpose of this pilgrimage. As you read these stories, see if you can find some answers to the following questions.

- What are some of the things Muslims do during Hajj?
- Why do Muslims go on pilgrimage to the Ka'ba in Makkah?

You could check your answers to these questions against some of the ideas given at the end of these stories.

Adam and Hawa

There is a reference to the Ka'ba in the Muslim story of Adam and Hawa, the first man and woman to live on earth. In the first part of that story, Adam and his wife, Hawa, disobeyed Allah. Because of this they had to leave the beautiful garden where Allah had put them. Here is the next part of the story which tells what happened to them after they left the garden.

Adam (peace be on him) comes to Arafat

After leaving the garden Adam (peace be on him) was sent to Mount Budh (in modern Sri Lanka) and Hawa (peace be on her) was sent to the Red Sea coast. Allah told Adam (peace be on him) to go to Bakka valley. Bakka was the early name of present Makkah. After travelling to various places Adam (peace be on him) saw the valley of Makkah where he found a throne that Allah had sent. He built a stone house round about it and called it Ka'ba. After this he went to Arafat and stood on a hill and prayed to Allah for forgiveness. Hawa (peace be on her) also had reached that place. They again met. That hill is still called Jabal-i-Rahman – the Hill of Mercy – because Allah forgave them both when Adam and Hawa (peace be on them) wept and prayed for forgiveness just before sunset.

Because of this story, many Muslims believe that the Ka'ba was the first building used for the worship of Allah. This story also explains why many Muslims go to Arafat on the ninth day of the Hajj and pray to Allah before sunset.

The second story is about the prophet Ibrahim. This story also helps us understand some of the things that Muslims do when they go on Hajj. It is a very long story, and part of it is told earlier in this book. Perhaps you remember how Ibrahim believed that Allah wanted him to sacrifice his son, Ismail, and how they resisted the temptation of Shaytan. Here are two more parts of the story. The first part is about something that happened before Ibrahim was told that he should sacrifice Ismail.

Ismail and the well of Zamzam

Ibrahim (peace be on him) married Sarah but they had no children. As he was growing older, with the permission of Sarah he married Hagar, their slave girl. He had a son by her. His name was Ismail. When Sarah saw that Ibrahim (peace be on him) was very fond of his son, she became jealous of Hagar. This made their life unhappy. Ibrahim (peace be on him) did not know what to do.

When Ismail was only a few months old Allah ordered Ibrahim (peace be on him) to go to Makkah (which was at that time known as Bakka) and leave Hagar and Ismail at that place. Ibrahim (peace be on him) brought them all the way from Canaan to Bakka. But they found a hilly, barren land. In that valley they saw a mound, the mound under which was hidden the broken house of Allah built by Adam (peace be on him). He did not see the house as it was covered with sand. He found the place lonely and dry, without any water. But he had to obey Allah. He left Hagar and Ismail with a bag of dates and a leather bottle full of water. When he was going away Hagar was surprised. She did not know that he would leave them like this. She asked him, 'O Ibrahim, where are you going, leaving us in this desert? There is no one here and nothing to eat or drink.'

He did not turn back. She then asked him, 'Has Allah ordered you to do this or are you doing it yourself?'

He said, 'It is Allah's command.'

'Then,' she said, 'He will not let us die.'

With firmness and courage she sat on a stone and prayed to Allah for help. Alone, all, all alone she sat.

She suckled the child and drank the water. But when there was no water left for her to drink she felt thirsty and her throat got very dry. She must get some water or she would die. The child was crying and she could not be away for very long. She rushed to the nearby hill (later on known as Safa) to see if there was any water or anyone anywhere to help her. She saw no one and she did not find any water.

Then she ran to the other hill (later on known as Marwah) and found nobody and saw no water. She ran seven times praying to Allah for help. Then she heard someone calling her. She looked at her son and saw an angel pointing at his feet. What joy! There she saw a fountain gushing out of the ground! There was water. She ran. She drank that water. She filled the bottle and dug a well and gave it the name of Zamzam.

Once again there is reference in this story to the Ka'ba. The part of this story which tells of Hagar's running seven times between the hills looking for water is also important for Muslims because it shows their belief that Allah always cares for those who obey him. The re-enacting of this story is also part of the ritual of the Hajj.

Many years after Ibrahim had been willing to sacrifice his son, Ismail, he returned to Makkah again to see his son. This part of the story tells of that visit and how Ibrahim and Ismail built the Ka'ba.

The rebuilding of the Ka'ba

Ibrahim (peace be on him) visited Makkah again. Ismail had then grown up and was an important man and a prophet. When Ibrahim (peace be on him) came to the place he could not find Hagar or Ismail. He met a young Jurhumi woman in a hut near where a few goats were grazing. The woman's name was Ri'lah, the daughter of Mudad ibn'Amn and the wife of Ismail. She told Ibrahim (peace be on him) that her husband had gone out hunting.

Ri'lah was very good to Ibrahim (peace be on him). She washed his hair and gave him meat to eat.

When Ibrahim (peace be on him) asked her about Hagar she said that she had died some years ago and that she was buried nearby.

When Ismail returned, Ibrahim (peace be on him) asked him to help him build Allah's house there. But where would they build it? They went out and waited for guidance from Allah. Then a dragon-shaped cloud came and its shadow fell on a large mound of earth. They started digging the ground and found to their surprise the ruins of the original house that Adam had built.

Here they raised new foundations and built a house of stone. No mortar was used. Stone was laid on stone. It had no roof.

While building the walls Ibrahim (peace be on him) had to stand on a piece of rock which Ismail had brought for him. The marks of his feet were left on this stone. Since they had no ladder Allah made the stone rise and move as the walls got higher and higher. Ibrahim (peace be on him) and Ismail completed building the Ka'ba. But they did not give it a roof.

Then they wanted to place a stone on the eastern corner from which they would start going round the Ka'ba. It is said that when Ismail

had gone out in search of a unique stone, the bright stone that was on the grave of Adam (peace be on him) in Mount Abu Qubais moved and fitted itself into that corner. It is this bright stone which has become black in the course of time, and is at present known as the Black Stone (Hajri Aswad). This stone is still in the easternmost corner of the Ka'ba.

After building the Ka'ba Ibrahim and Ismail prayed to Allah. Ibrahim (peace be on him) said, 'O Allah, make this town a secure town. I have placed my child here and his children will remain here. Give food and fruits to the believer.' Allah said, 'Even the unbelievers will enjoy life here and get food here but they will suffer in the after-life.'

They also prayed, 'O our Lord, accept our prayers, guide us so that we submit to you. Show us the way. Be merciful to us. Raise from our children people who will believe in You and obey You. Raise up a messenger from these people. Surely You are Mighty and Wise.'

Ibrahim (peace be on him) and Ismail went round the Ka'ba seven times. Then they ran seven times to As-Safa and Al-Marwah to commemorate what Hagar had done when Ismail was a little baby. Finally, Ibrahim (peace be on him) said goodbye to Ismail, his beloved son, and went back to Canaan.

During the Hajj, most of the pilgrims try to follow the example of Ibrahim and Ismail. They may kiss the stone in the eastern corner of the Ka'ba and then walk around the building seven times.

Our last story tells of an event towards the end of Muhammad's life. It too gives us an idea of what Muslims do today, when they go on the Hajj.

Muhammad's last pilgrimage

One year, when Muhammad was still living in Medina, it was proclaimed that the Prophet (peace be on him) would be going to Makkah. The Muslims flocked to Medina from all over Arabia to join him on his journey to the Ka'ba. As the tribes arrived they camped around the city until they finally numbered more than thirty thousand. The Prophet (peace be on him) went out with his family and friends to meet them and to lead them on the pilgrimage, but before setting off, he led all the Muslims in prayer. After the prayers, the Prophet (peace be on him) got on his camel and headed towards Makkah followed by the pilgrims, all of whom, for the first time in centuries, worshipped Allah, the One God.

Throughout the journey the Muslims repeated a prayer taught to them by the Prophet (peace be on him), which he in turn had received from the Archangel Gabriel. This prayer, the Talbiyah, has been part of the Hajj ritual ever since.

Here I am, O Allah, at Thy service. Here I am,
Thou art without partner, here I am. All Praise and blessings are thine, and Dominion! Thou art without partner!

When they reached the Ka'ba the Prophet (peace be on him) stood before it in prayer, then he and all the Muslims walked around it seven times saying their prayer aloud. Next, just as Ibrahim (peace be on him) had done, they went towards the Mount of Mercy at Arafat which the Prophet (peace be on him) ascended on a camel.

From the mountain he led the people in prayer and then spoke to them as they stood assembled on the vast plain below. What the Prophet (peace be on him) said is known as the 'Farewell Sermon', because it was the last speech the Prophet (peace be on him) made before he died. He said, 'Surely you will meet your Lord and He will question you about your works.' He asked the Muslims to take their guidance from the Qur'an and from his own example. This, he said, was the best way to live. He ordered them to cease living in the way they had before Islam. Revenge, one of the oldest traditions in Arabia, was ended forever; lending money at interest was prohibited; property was to be respected. Things which previously were forbidden during the four sacred months of the year were now forbidden at all times. He then commanded, 'Know that every Muslim is a Muslim's brother,' which was a completely new idea to the tribes who had so often quarrelled in the past. He also said, 'Allah has given everyone his due – exactly what each one deserves.' After each point the Prophet (peace be on him) asked, 'Have I explained it well? Is it perfectly clear?'

Everyone answered, 'Yes.' For these were the people who would have to pass on the Prophet's message and instructions to those who were unable to be present that day and to future generations.

The Prophet (peace be on him) said, 'I have left you two things. If you hold on to them you will be saved. They are Allah's Book and the words of your Prophet.' He then asked, 'Have I not conveyed the message?'

The multitude shouted out, 'By Allah, yes!'

The Prophet (peace be on him) ended, 'O Allah! Bear witness to that.'

Many Muslims started to shed tears, knowing that if the Prophet (peace be on him) had completed his message, his life must be near its end.

The rituals of the Hajj

These stories may have given you some idea of what most of the pilgrims do on the Hajj.

Here are seven of the most important ceremonies which each of the pilgrims may perform during the Hajj. Each of these ceremonies is intended to express some of the central beliefs of Islam. Many of the pilgrims also believe that by joining in these ceremonies, they are helped to live better lives as Muslims.

WEARING IHRAM
Ihram for men consists of putting on two sheets of unsewn white cloth. For women it consists of wearing clean, plain clothes.

At least three Islamic beliefs are symbolised by wearing this simple form of dress.

- All Muslims are equal before Allah.
- All Muslims are humble servants of Allah.
- Material things do not have any lasting value.

GOING AROUND THE KA'BA SEVEN TIMES
This ceremony reminds the pilgrims of the practice of Ibrahim, Ismail and Muhammad. It expresses their belief that the Ka'ba is the very first place built on earth for the worship of Allah. It also shows the Muslim belief that Makkah is the world's centre for belief in one God.

A FAST WALK OR RUN BETWEEN AS-SAFA AND AL-MARWAH

When they join in this walk or run, pilgrims are reminded of Hagar's great concern for Ismail, when they were left in the desert without water. It also reminds them of their belief that Allah cares for and bestows favour on those who submit themselves in obedience to his will.

VISITING AND STAYING AT SUCH PLACES AS ARAFAT

Many Muslims believe that their faith in and obedience to Allah are strengthened when they visit these places. They are the traditional spots where the will of Allah was revealed to some of the prophets, especially Muhammad. To be in the actual places where this happened is believed to give greater spiritual strength.

THROWING STONES AT THREE PLACES IN MINA

The ritual performance of this part of the Ibrahim and Ismail story reminds the pilgrims of their belief in Shaytan and in the power of evil. Muslims believe that they must always be on their guard to resist evil and to obey Allah.

CUTTING OR SHORTENING HAIR

Towards the end of the Hajj many Muslim men have their heads shaved or at least have their hair cut very short. This too is an expression of their belief that during the Hajj they are very close to Allah. All physical appearances and outward show give way to complete devotion and submission to Allah.

SACRIFICE OF AN ANIMAL

Many of the pilgrims offer a sheep, a goat or perhaps a camel, as a sacrifice on the tenth day of the month of Dhu'l Hijjah. Again this recalls a part of the Ibrahim and Ismail story. Many pilgrims try to do this at Mina, which is regarded as the traditional spot where Ibrahim eventually sacrificed the ram instead of Ismail. This sacrifice reminds them that they must be ready to give up everything for Allah.

Muslims who go on this pilgrimage to Makkah, at least once in their lifetime, are given a special title. Men are called Hajji and women who complete the pilgrimage are called Hajja. These people feel that it is a great privilege and honour to have completed the pilgrimage and they may be treated with great respect within the Muslim community. More importantly, most of them believe that the pilgrimage has strengthened their personal faith in Allah. They may also feel better able to carry out the duties and responsibilities of living as Muslims.

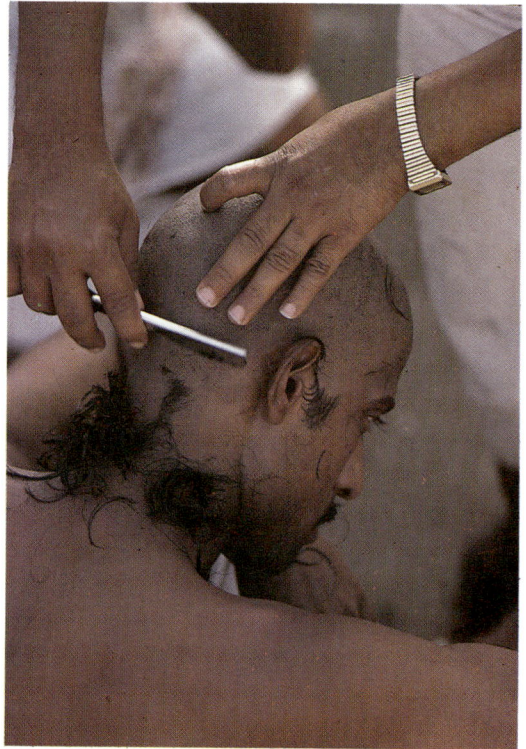

Personal standards and stances

By now you will know something about the religion of Islam. It is a way of life for millions of people and there are Muslims in almost every country of the world. We must never forget that Islam is made up of individuals. All of these people find their own ways of being a Muslim. All Muslims do not believe or do exactly the same thing in exactly the same way.

As well as expressing their beliefs through religious activities, Muslims try to apply their religion to their personal standards of behaviour and their attitudes to moral and social issues.

As you know, Muslims sum up the whole of their faith in the words of the Shahadah. The regular and sincere declaration of this belief is the first of the five duties of a Muslim.

لَا إِلَهَ إِلَّا اللَّهُ مُحَمَّدٌ رَسُولُ اللَّهِ

There is no god but Allah, Muhammad is the Messenger of Allah.

These words provide the basic principles by which Muslims deal with such difficult social and moral issues as crime, poverty, war, cruelty, unemployment, terrorism, abortion, organ transplants, divorce, conservation and animal rights.

The religion of Islam teaches that the Qur'an sets out a whole way of life and lays down many rules which, if obeyed, lead to a truly Muslim lifestyle. The Qur'an is therefore the most important source of guidance for all Muslims seeking to live their personal lives in accordance with the will of Allah.

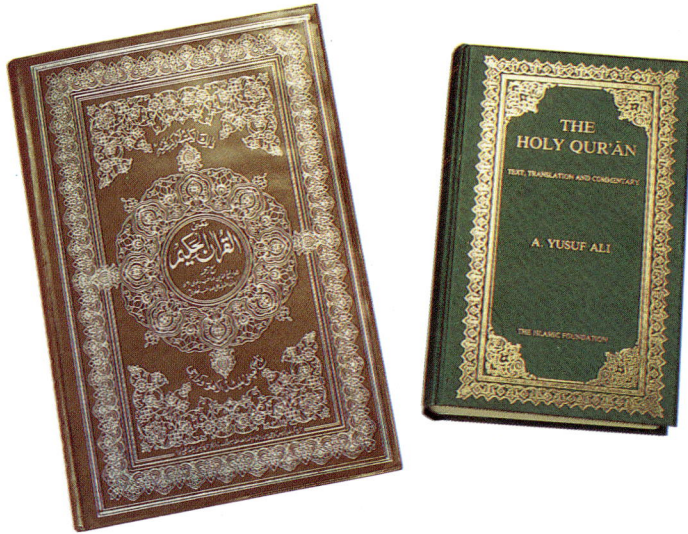

Muslims are also taught that the practice of the Prophet Muhammad is another essential source of guidance for all people who want to live as Muslims. The practices of the Prophet are known as Sunnah and the records of these are found in a large set of books known as the Hadith.

Here is one important passage from the Qur'an which many Muslims look to for guidance in their efforts to live a truly Muslim lifestyle. Muslims believe that these guidelines are as relevant today as they were when Muhammad first received them and recited them.

O Muhammad, say to them, "Come, I will recite what limits your Lord has set for you." (He has enjoined:) That you should not set up anything as a partner with Him, and you should treat your parents kindly, and you should not kill your children for fear of poverty, for We provide sustenance for you and will provide sustenance for them also, and you should not go near indecent things whether they be open or hidden, and you should not kill any living being whom Allah has forbidden to kill except by right. These are the things which He has enjoined on you: it may be that you use your common sense..And He has enjoined: that you should not go near the property of an orphan except in the best way, until he reaches his maturity, and you should use a full measure and a just balance. We charge every person only with that much responsibility that he can bear, and whatever you say should be just, even if it is concerning your own relatives, and you should fulfill your covenant with Allah. Allah has enjoined these things on you so that you may follow the admonition.

Surah 6:151, 152

قُلْ تَعَالَوْاْ أَتْلُ مَا حَرَّمَ رَبُّكُمْ عَلَيْكُمْ أَلَّا تُشْرِكُواْ بِهِ شَيْئًا وَبِٱلْوَٰلِدَيْنِ إِحْسَٰنًا وَلَا تَقْتُلُوٓاْ أَوْلَٰدَكُم مِّنْ إِمْلَٰقٍ نَّحْنُ نَرْزُقُكُمْ وَإِيَّاهُمْ وَلَا تَقْرَبُواْ ٱلْفَوَٰحِشَ مَا ظَهَرَ مِنْهَا وَمَا بَطَنَ وَلَا تَقْتُلُواْ ٱلنَّفْسَ ٱلَّتِى حَرَّمَ ٱللَّهُ إِلَّا بِٱلْحَقِّ ذَٰلِكُمْ وَصَّىٰكُم بِهِ لَعَلَّكُمْ تَعْقِلُونَ

وَلَا تَقْرَبُواْ مَالَ ٱلْيَتِيمِ إِلَّا بِٱلَّتِى هِىَ أَحْسَنُ حَتَّىٰ يَبْلُغَ أَشُدَّهُ وَأَوْفُواْ ٱلْكَيْلَ وَٱلْمِيزَانَ بِٱلْقِسْطِ لَا نُكَلِّفُ نَفْسًا إِلَّا وُسْعَهَا وَإِذَا قُلْتُمْ فَٱعْدِلُواْ وَلَوْ كَانَ ذَا قُرْبَىٰ وَبِعَهْدِ ٱللَّهِ أَوْفُواْ ذَٰلِكُمْ وَصَّىٰكُم بِهِ لَعَلَّكُمْ تَذَكَّرُونَ

Which of the general ideas about good living in this passage from the Qur'an match your personal beliefs about how people should live today?

Along with such general principles as being good to parents, not killing people 'except by right' and speaking justly, the Qur'an also contains some very specific commandments for Muslims to follow.

Here are three examples. As you read these quotations from the Qur'an, see which, if any, of the commands come close to some of your personal beliefs and standards.

O Prophet, enjoin the Believing men to restrain their gaze and guard their private parts. This is a more righteous way for them: Allah has knowledge of whatever they do.

And O Prophet, enjoin the Believing women to restrain their gaze and guard their private parts and not to display their adornment except that which is displayed of itself, and to draw their veils over their bosoms and not to display their adornment except before their husbands, their fathers, the fathers of their husbands, their sons and the sons of their husbands (from other wives), their brothers, their brothers' sons, their sisters' sons, their female associates and those in their possession and male attendants incapable of sex desire and those boys who have not yet attained knowledge of sex matters concerning women; also forbid them to stamp their feet on the ground lest their hidden ornaments should be displayed.

O Believers, turn all together towards Allah: it is expected that you will attain true success.

Surah 24:30, 31

قُل لِّلْمُؤْمِنِينَ يَغُضُّوا مِنْ أَبْصَرِهِمْ وَيَحْفَظُوا فُرُوجَهُمْ ذَلِكَ أَزْكَىٰ لَهُمْ إِنَّ ٱللَّهَ خَبِيرٌ بِمَا يَصْنَعُونَ

وَقُل لِّلْمُؤْمِنَتِ يَغْضُضْنَ مِنْ أَبْصَرِهِنَّ وَيَحْفَظْنَ فُرُوجَهُنَّ وَلَا يُبْدِينَ زِينَتَهُنَّ إِلَّا مَا ظَهَرَ مِنْهَا وَلْيَضْرِبْنَ

بِخُمُرِهِنَّ عَلَىٰ جُيُوبِهِنَّ وَلَا يُبْدِينَ زِينَتَهُنَّ إِلَّا لِبُعُولَتِهِنَّ أَوْ ءَابَآئِهِنَّ أَوْ ءَابَآءِ بُعُولَتِهِنَّ أَوْ أَبْنَآئِهِنَّ أَوْ أَبْنَآءِ بُعُولَتِهِنَّ أَوْ إِخْوَٰنِهِنَّ أَوْ بَنِىٓ إِخْوَٰنِهِنَّ أَوْ بَنِىٓ أَخَوَٰتِهِنَّ أَوْ نِسَآئِهِنَّ أَوْ مَا مَلَكَتْ أَيْمَٰنُهُنَّ أَوِ ٱلتَّٰبِعِينَ غَيْرِ أُوْلِى ٱلْإِرْبَةِ مِنَ ٱلرِّجَالِ أَوِ ٱلطِّفْلِ ٱلَّذِينَ لَمْ يَظْهَرُوا عَلَىٰ عَوْرَٰتِ ٱلنِّسَآءِ وَلَا يَضْرِبْنَ بِأَرْجُلِهِنَّ لِيُعْلَمَ مَا يُخْفِينَ مِن زِينَتِهِنَّ وَتُوبُوٓا إِلَى ٱللَّهِ جَمِيعًا أَيُّهَ ٱلْمُؤْمِنُونَ لَعَلَّكُمْ تُفْلِحُونَ

Do not even go near fornication for it is a very indecent thing and a very evil way.

Surah 17:32

وَلَا تَقْرَبُوا ٱلزِّنَىٰٓ إِنَّهُ كَانَ فَٰحِشَةً وَسَآءَ سَبِيلًا

O Believers, wine, gambling, (ungodly) shrines and divining devices are all abominable works of Shaytan: therefore refrain from these so that you may attain true success. Indeed Shaytan intends to sow enmity and hatred among you by means of wine and gambling, and to prevent you from the remembrance of Allah and from Salah. Will you not, therefore, abstain from these things?

Surah 5:90,91

يَٰٓأَيُّهَا ٱلَّذِينَ ءَامَنُوٓا إِنَّمَا ٱلْخَمْرُ وَٱلْمَيْسِرُ وَٱلْأَنصَابُ وَٱلْأَزْلَٰمُ رِجْسٌ مِّنْ عَمَلِ ٱلشَّيْطَٰنِ فَٱجْتَنِبُوهُ لَعَلَّكُمْ تُفْلِحُونَ

إِنَّمَا يُرِيدُ ٱلشَّيْطَٰنُ أَن يُوقِعَ بَيْنَكُمُ ٱلْعَدَٰوَةَ وَٱلْبَغْضَآءَ فِى ٱلْخَمْرِ وَٱلْمَيْسِرِ وَيَصُدَّكُمْ عَن ذِكْرِ ٱللَّهِ وَعَنِ ٱلصَّلَوٰةِ فَهَلْ أَنتُم مُّنتَهُونَ

One of the most popular collections of some of the Sunnah is known as *The Forty Hadith*. It too was written a long time ago and provides Muslims with a record of some of the Prophet's sayings and practice.

Again, as you read this passage, see if there is any similarity between your ideas and beliefs about personal values and standards of behaviour and those contained in these verses.

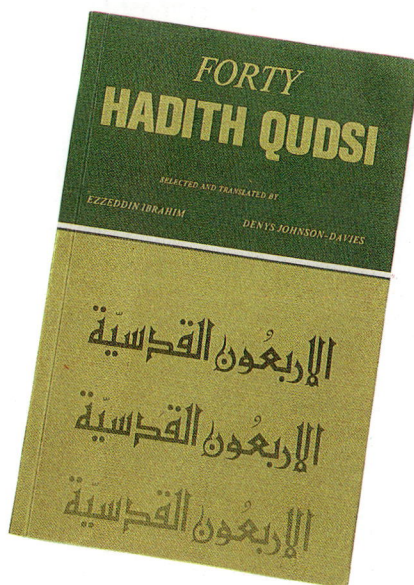

On the authority of Abu Huraira (may Allah be pleased with him), who said: The Messenger of Allah (may the blessings and peace of Allah be upon him) said:

Do not envy one another; do not inflate prices one to another; do not hate one another; do not turn away from one another; and do not undercut one another, but be you, O servants of Allah, brothers. A Muslim is the brother of a Muslim: he neither oppresses him nor does he fail him, he neither lies to him nor does he hold him in contempt. Piety is right here – and he pointed to his breast three times. It is evil enough for a man to hold his brother Muslim in contempt. The whole of a Muslim for another Muslim is inviolable: his blood, his property, and his honour.

eachers

The material in this book is intended to help young people learn about Muslims. Islamic practices and beliefs are described clearly and without any assumptions being made about any teacher's or pupil's acceptance of the Islamic religion now or in the future.

Clearly one book cannot deal with every aspect of Islam. This book, along with others in the set, points to important features of Islam and gives pupils some clear guidelines for continuing their exploration of this religion within the context of R.E. in schools.

This book is the third in a set of four books. It is intended for use with pupils aged 11–14 years, and is therefore best suited for use in lower secondary R.E. courses.

There are three parts to this book. Part One extends pupils' understanding of important features of Muslim communities and the beliefs they express. Part Two focusses on Muslim family life. In Part Three pupils are helped to explore some of the ways in which individual Muslims apply their beliefs to their own personal lives. The three parts are indicated by colour coding: pink for Part One, blue for Part Two, yellow for Part Three. The coloured box round each page number shows which part the page is in.

Because this book is part of a structured and developmental scheme, some knowledge of Islam is assumed. However, some teachers may decide that a particular group of pupils does not have the assumed knowledge and is therefore not ready to proceed with this book. They may well decide that at least some preparatory work, using Book 2 in this set, is necessary.

Content overview of the pupils' books
The four pupils' books in this series are designed to help pupils develop an understanding of Islam as a world religion. Each book deals with different aspects of Islamic practices, beliefs and experiences.

The diagrammatic presentation below indicates the content of each book and shows how pupils are helped to build up, in a progressive way from 7–16, their knowledge and understanding of this religion. The shaded areas in the circles indicate the aspects of Islam dealt with in particular books.

A more detailed explanation of this way of distributing the subject matter across the four books is given in the teacher's books, *How do I teach R.E.?* and *Islam*.

MUSLIMS 1
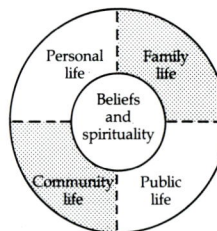

MUSLIMS 2
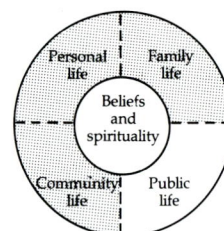

MUSLIMS 3
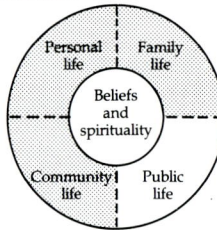

MUSLIMS 4
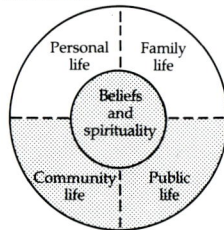

Other materials in this Project
Teachers using this book with lower secondary pupils must realise that it is only one resource item designed to meet one specific aspect of the pupils' experience of R.E. – learning about Muslims. To expand the range of classroom activities designed to meet this need, a **photopack**, with additional pictures and information, is also available.

Teachers using these resources are strongly recommended to refer to the two teacher's books:
How do I teach R.E.? – the main Project manual.
Islam – a source book and guide to the teaching of this religion.

Books and photopacks relating to other religious traditions and various Life Themes are also part of **The Westhill Project R.E. 5–16.**

64